The Baby-sitters

"I am going out,"
said the crocodile
to her baby.
"The baby-sitters
will look after you."

2

"Remember,"
said the crocodile.
"No snip-snap!"

3

The giraffe looked after
the baby crocodile.

Snip-snap!

4

Snip-Snap!

The hippopotamus
looked after
the baby crocodile.

Snip-snap!

Snip-snap!

The tiger looked after
the baby crocodile.

Snip-snap!

6

The monkey looked after
the baby crocodile.

"I looked after your baby,"
said the monkey
to the crocodile.
"**No** snip-snap."

8

The Knight
and the Dragon

"I am looking for the dragon," said the knight.

10

"It is not here,"
said the woman.

11

"I am looking
for the dragon,"
said the knight.

12

"It is not here," said the boy.

13

"Are you looking for the dragon?" said the bird.

"Yes," said the knight. "Where is it?"

The bird laughed
and laughed.
"Ha-ha! Ha-ha! Ha-ha!"

"Please," said the knight.
"Will you help me look
for the dragon?"

Pirate Pete's Treasure

Pirate Pete put the treasure in a sack.

He put the sack in a chest.

He put the chest in a hole.

He put stones in the hole.

Pirate Pete went away.
"Ha, ha!" said Pirate Pete.
"No one will find
my treasure!"

Pirate Pete came back.
He looked and looked.

"I cannot find my treasure!"